TRY NOT TO LAUGH CHALLENGE

Sleepover Party

Joke Book

D1115669

Howling Moon Books

Try Not to Laugh Challenge!

Rules:

Pick your team, or go one on one.

Sit across from each other & make eye contact.

Take turns reading jokes to each other.

You can make silly faces, funny sound effects, etc.

When your opponent laughs, you get a point!

First team to win 3 points, **Wins!**

Telling Jokes Builds Confident Kids, & Laughter Makes Everyone Happy!

Why should you invite a llama
to a slumber party?

Because they are a llama fun!

Why did the girl want to build
her pillow fort next to the
nightlight?

Because she was a light sleeper!

Why was the girl taking so
many pictures of herself?

She had no selfie control!

What is the difference between
a sleepover in New York and
a sleepover in California?

About 3,000 miles!

Why did the girl want to
sleep on the unicorn pool float?

She wanted to drift off to sleep!

What is the best kind of ship
to be on?

A friend-ship!

What do cats bring to sleepovers?

Slip-purrs!

Why are waffles better than pancakes?

Waffles have their own built-in syrup holders!

How do you get everyone to listen to you at a camp slumber party?

Yell "At-TENT-ion"!

What kind of game do beavers like to play?

Wood you rather!

Why doesn't a clock ever sleep?

Because it tocks too much!

What is a unicorn's favorite party game?

Don't Step in the Rainbow Poop!

Why did the girl sleepwalk?

She was following her dreams!

How do you get ready for a
scary ghost story?

Fasten your sheet belt!

When do ghosts eat breakfast?

In the moaning!

When does a unicorn sing Happy Birthday?

Whinney wants to!

Why don't gnomes go to sleepovers?

Because they always get gnome-sick!

What hangs around the birthday
party after it's over?

A birthday banner!

Why aren't there many popcorn
jokes?

Because they are pretty corny!

What kind of puzzles can make
you mad?

Cross-word puzzles!

Did you hear about the doughnut sleepover?

They stayed up the HOLE night!

What kind of flowers shouldn't you invite to a sleepover?

Morning glories!

Why were the friendship bracelets hard to tie together?

Knot sure!

When is it dangerous to surf the net?

Shark week!

Why do trees have so many friends at their parties?

They branch out!

Why shouldn't you let Elsa
walk your dog?

Because she will "Let it Go"!

What kind of chips do
doughnuts like?

Glaze potato chips!
(Lays)

Where do dogs go when they play
hide and seek?

The roof!

Knock knock.
Who's there?
Doughnut.
Doughnut who?

Doughnut open your presents
until we sing Happy Birthday!

How many skunks does it take
to stink up a sleepover party?

A phew!

What superhero likes to play question games on her birthday?

Wonder Woman!

Why do mermaids like to tell stories?

Because they have long tails!

What happens when you eat cookies in your pillow fort?

You will have a crummy night's sleep!

Where do caticorns buy their doughnuts?

Hole Foods!

Why are caticorns good at video games?

Because they have nine lives!

How did we know the slumber party
was a hit?

It was an overnight success!

Did you hear the joke about
the sleeping bag?

It hasn't been rolled out yet!

Why can't you wake up trees
at a sleepover party?

Because they sleep like logs!

Have you ever heard of
birthday toilet paper?

It's a rip off!

Knock knock.
Who's there?
Hugo.
Hugo who?

Hugo Girl!

What kind of cheese do dogs like
on their pizza?

Mutts-arella!

How do kids with poison ivy
bake homemade birthday
cookies?

They start from scratch!

Why did the Statue of Liberty
go to the doctor?

Her arm was sore!

Why is a mermaid fun at
a party?

She's always fishing around for
new games!

What mermaids live at the
bottom of the ocean?

A deep she-fish!

Knock knock.
Who's there?
Bacon.
Bacon who?

I am bacon muffins for
breakfast!

What kind of drinks do you have
at a pool party?

Ice cream floats!

Who should you invite to your
dance party?

The Boogeyman!

What do you need to ride a unicorn in space?

A saddle-lite!

Why are unicorns terrible dancers?

Because they have two left feet!

Knock knock.
Who's there?
Venice
Venice who?

Venice is it time to paint
our nails?

What time is it when a ghost
is in your sleeping bag?

Time to get a new sleeping bag!

Where do ghosts sleep at
a slumber party?

On a scare mattress!

What did the pizza say at
the birthday sleepover party?

Have a slice birthday!

Why do soccer players have
trouble with finger food?

Because they keep thinking
that they can't use their hands!

Why doesn't Snow White like
social media?

She only has 7 followers!

Where do you get a
S'more-Frappe on the moon?

Starbucks!

How do you make a baby
computer cry?

Delete his cookies!

How do the kids on the moon
keep in touch with their family?

Spacebook!

What kind of pasta do you serve
at a Halloween sleepover?

Fettucini alfraido!

What did the little owl want
to do at the slumber party?

Stay up owl night!

What do dogs wear at a
sleepover party?

Paw-jamas!

Where do you post photos of
your spa sleepover party?

Insta-glam!

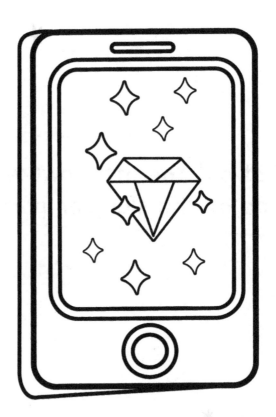

We heard the kids were having
fun at the beach party.

Surf far, surf good!

Why did the birthday candles
need a vacation?

They were burnt out!

What slumber party game do
parents wish their kids
would not play?

The Try NOT to Sleep Challenge!

What kind of pasta grants
three wishes?

Fettu-genie!

What group of young girls likes
to dance?

The Twirl Scouts!

How did Pegasus find his way to
the sleepover party?

He just winged it!

Why can't you sneak up on a
telescope?

It can see you coming
a million miles away!

Which dinosaur should you never
invite to your slumber party?

Tyranno-snore-us Rex!

Why were the girls tip toeing
around the room at the
sleepover party?

Because the room was full
of sleeping bags!

What is a frog's favorite party game?

The Croaky Pokey!

What kind of dance might you do at a beach party?

The Tan-go!

What sea animal stays up late?

A starfish!

What are princess farts made of?

Royal gas!

Knock knock.
Who's there?
Tail.
Tail who?

Tail everyone it's time for
a pillow fight!

Why did the musician want to
sit in the rocking chair?

Because she wanted to
Rock and Roll!

What do cheerleaders eat
for breakfast?

Cheerios!

Why did the kid eat the party quiz?

Someone said it was a piece of cake!

Why are unicorns good at hide and go seek?

They like to poke around!

What do you call a funny movie
in outer space?

A comet-y!

Knock knock.
Who's there?
Wanda.
Wanda who?

Wanda build pillow forts now?

How did the girls at the sleepover
figure out how to make spaghetti?

They used their noodle!

Why didn't the kids
trust the bunk bed ladder?

Because it was always up
to something!

What do you call a dog that likes
bubble baths?

A Shampoodle!

Why were the stargazers having a good time at the party?

Because things were looking up!

Why couldn't the bicycles stay awake at the slumber party?

Because they were two-tired!

Why don't Pterodactyls wake anyone up when they go to the bathroom?

Because their P is silent!

Why did Elsa's video game stop playing?

It froze!

Why should you invite a cat to birthday parties?

In case you need a first aid kitty!

What do you do with a chatty sleeping bag?

Tell it to zip it!

The sleepover party wondered why it was taking so long for the sun to rise.

Then it dawned on them!

Why did the girls stand on their chairs to sing Happy Birthday?

They wanted to hit the high notes!

Knock knock.
Who's there?
Dishes.
Dishes who?

Dishes going to be a great slumber party!

Why did the kids put sugar under their pillows?

Because they wanted sweet dreams!

What special breakfast did the
unicorn make for the party?

Breakfast glitz!
(grits)

Knock knock.
Who's there?
Muffin.
Muffin who?

Muffin in this world will
keep me from having
a s'more!

What did the angry ghost
say to her boyfriend?

Get a life!

What woke up everyone at the
sleepover party?

The crack of dawn!

Knock knock.
Who's there?
Rita
Rita who?

Rita a book if you can't fall
asleep!

How do you make a milkshake?

Tell it a ghost story!

Why did the chocolate eclair go to the dentist?

It lost its filling!

What happens to little flashlights?

They glow up!

What kind of backpack is always tired?

A knapsack!

How did the girls get to the
beach so fast?

They took a shore cut!

Knock knock.
Who's there?
Seaweed.
Seaweed who?

Sea, weed better go swimming
before the sun goes down!

What do scuba divers wear to bed?

Snore-kels!

Did you hear about the burrito joke?

Never mind, it's too cheesy!

Why did the girl put her speakers next to the ice bucket?

She wanted to play cool music!

What happened when the girl dropped her iphone in the swimming pool?

It started syncing!

How do mermaids like
their hamburgers cooked?

Whale done!

Knock knock.
Who's there?
Sadie.
Sadie who?

Sadie word and I'll sing
Party in the USA!

What do pirates have
for breakfast?

Boatmeal!

Why is a sloth an expert sleeper?

He is so good at it, he can do it with his eyes shut!

What kind of phone do cheerleaders use?

A mega-phone!

Where do top secret spy books like to sleep?

Under their covers!

What do you do if a unicorn
comes to your sleepover party?

Give her some unicorn slippers!

Why do unicorns run in bed?

Because they are fast asleep!

What do you call a fairy who is in charge of fixing things?

Tinkerbell!

What lights up a sports stadium?

A soccer match!

When is a gymnast like a judge?

When she sits on the bench!

In what position do ghosts sleep?

Horror-zontal!

Knock, knock.
Who's there?
Wayne.
Wayne who?

Wayne are we going to play
M.A.S.H.?

How do you talk to ghosts?

You use scary words!

Why did the kid get heartburn from eating a piece of birthday cake?

He left the candles on!

What do jokesters eat for breakfast?

Pun-cakes!

Why did the soccer ball quit the team?

It was tired of being kicked around!

What do you call a spy
in a bubble bath?

Bubble 07!

What kind of bedtime books do
you read to a Jack-in-the-Box?

Pop-up books!

Why were the mushrooms invited
to the slumber party?

Because they are such fungis!

Why did the girl want a king sized bed?

She had big dreams!

What is a gymnast's motto?

Chalky hair, don't care!

Why did the girl wish she was younger?

She wanted to sleep like a baby!

What kind of make-up does
a ghost use?

Mas-scare-a.

Why can't you give a balloon to
Elsa for her birthday?

Because she will "Let it Go"!

Why didn't Snow White go
to New York City?

She didn't want to take a bite
of the Big Apple!

What happened to the little shark
who was invited to two parties
on the same day?

He was stuck between a rock
and a shark place!

What did the mom shark say
to her misbehaving children?

Go ahead, Mako my day!

How do you know if your mascara
is mad?

It will lash out at you!

What frozen desserts do you serve
at a unicorn's birthday party?

Ice cream uni-cones!

What happened when the girls
tried vanishing cream at the
spa party?

Nobody knows!

Why do ghosts have really
good hearing?

Because they are very ear-rie!

Why did the birthday candles have
a great time at the party?

Because they were blown away!

How did the skunk get to
the birthday party?

On her odorcycle!

What game does the Tooth Fairy play at sleepover parties?

Tooth or Dare!

How is milk like the speed of light?

Because it's pasteurized before you see it!

Why didn't the girl want a camping slumber party?

Because it's in-tents!

What was wrong with the story about a caticorn who had a broken horn?

It didn't have a point!

The blush, mascara and eye shadow were fighting at the party...

It was okay, they always makeup!

Why don't dragons like sleepover parties?

Because they don't like parties that drag-on!

Why are aliens on the moon bald?

No air!
(no hair)

When is the only time you can get rid of a dragon?

The knight shift!

When is it time to get some
sleep at the party?

Snore o'clock!

When is it time to hit the pool
at the party?

Dive o'clock!

When is it time to do
some yoga at the party?

Zen o'clock!

Why did the gymnasts put
extra salt on their food?

So they could do summer-salts!

Why were the balloons tired
after the slumber party?

Because they stayed up all night!

What is it called when a dinosaur
gets a goal?

A dino-score!

The kids couldn't figure out
how to hook up to the zipline.

Then it clicked!

Why didn't the teddy bear
come to the sleepover?

He was all stuffed up!

What song does Elsa sing to
her plants?

Let it Grow!

Why wouldn't the toilet paper
stop telling jokes?

Because it was on a roll!

Why did the little tree leave the
party early?

It was time to leaf!

Why couldn't the laptop get
into the house?

It didn't have the right key!

What nail polish takes forever to dry?

Snail polish!

What kind of bath do hedgehogs avoid?

A bubble bath!

How do you pay for pizza?

With pizza dough!

Where do unicorn cookies sleep?

On a cookie sheet!

Why doesn't Sleeping Beauty go to slumber parties?

She never gets her beauty sleep!

What do eggs do for fun at parties?

Kare-yolkie!

Why do good friends like to play
the Limbo?

They don't mind bending over
backwards for each other!

Do pickles enjoy their friends?

Yup, they relish the moments!

What did the potato say
when it was wrapped with foil
and put on the grill?

"Foiled again"!

What happens if you eat too
much chocolate candy?

You can turn into a cocoa-nut!

Why didn't the little mermaid like
the taste-testing challenge?

Because she is a fin-icky eater!

Why does Peter Pan have to wait for breakfast to have his birthday cake?

Because it's a pan-cake!

What do you always get on your birthday?

A year older!

Why are ballerinas ready for anything?

Because they are always on their toes!

Did you hear about the letter that got lost at the post office?

Never mind, you won't get it!

Why is Snow White afraid of the evil Queen?

Because she is a bad apple!

Did the little mermaid enjoy her slumber party?

She had a whale of a time!

What do llamas eat for lunch?

Llama-bles!

What special treats do unicorns love?

Pop-corn balls!

The kids had german sausages instead of hot dogs at the party.

It was the Wurst!

Why should you do laundry at a party?

Because it's loads of fun!

Why are the jokes about
Neverland so funny?

They never get old!

Where does Tinkerbell go to
buy a puppy?

The Littlest Pet Shop!

Why do you want the fireflies
in charge of making breakfast?

Because they are lightning fast!

Who is the most famous pig
in the art world?

Pigcasso!

What do you call a bathtub fart?

A bath bomb!

What kind of kids can't wear
flip flops?

Kids that have a lactose problem!
(lack toes)

Did you hear about the shark
sleepover party?

It was fin-tastic!

Why was Cinderella terrible at tap dancing?

She kept losing her shoes!

What do you call an elf that plays lacrosse?

A shortie!

How do you catch a fairy?

By the fairy-tale!

What kind of birthday party do gymnasts like?

A trampoline party!

Where do ghosts post their videos?

BooTube!

What do ghosts like on their bagels?

Scream cheese!

How does a mermaid find her way to the slumber party?

Otter-pilot!

What did the journal say to the pen?

Write on!

Why do people write on birthday cakes?

Because birthday kids want to have their cake and read it too!

What do you sing to a poop emoji on his birthday?

Happy Birthday to Poo!

Who are the best soccer players?

The players who keep their head
in the game!

Why did the vegetarian quit the
swim team?

She doesn't like meets!

Why does the sloth love
sleeping so much?

It is his dream job!

The girls lost their mood rings at the slumber party.

They weren't sure how they felt about that!

Who is on the cover of a ghost beauty magazine?

The cover ghoul!

Did you hear about the fruit that got married?

They lived Apple-y ever after!

Knock, knock.
Who's there?
Dozen.
Dozen who?

Dozen everyone want to
stay up all night?!

Knock, knock.
Who's there?
Herd.
Herd who?

I herd that we are having
s'mores tonight!

What do deer like to eat for breakfast?

Doe-nuts!

What do you say about singing karaoke with a friend?

Just Duet!

What happens when movie stars fight?

Star Wars!

Where did the cheerleader want
to have her sleepover party?

At the Great Pyramid!

How do you slice Tiramisu?

With a knife, it is a piece
of cake!

Why did the girl put gel pens
in her sleeping bag?

So she could dream in color!

Why did the banana leave
the sleepover party early?

It wasn't peeling well!

How do jokesters like their eggs?

Funny side up!

What do unicorns like to play at sleepover parties?

Apples to Apples!

What is a ballerina's favorite number?

Two two!

Why was the swimmer so slow?

She was doing the crawl!

Which sport is angry?

La-crosse!

How does a robot eat guacamole?

With micro-chips!

What do you call two friends who like to gift each other flowers?

Best Buds!

How do you get the sleepover
party to fall asleep?

Give them PiZZZZZZa!

What do you give a monster if he
comes to your sleepover?

Big slippers!

What do mermaids post on Instagram?

Shellfies!

What game would the Statue of Liberty like to play?

Pass the torch!

Did you hear about the family
that went to Paris to see
the famous tower?

They got an Eiffel!

Why do ghosts make such good
cheerleaders?

They are full of spirit!

What did the kids say about
the party cheese platter?

Looking Gouda!

What snack do you promise
to give in exchange for
a group picture?

"Cheese"-its!

Who sets the rules for a
ghost's slumber party?

The transparents!

What do ghosts wear on their nails?

Nail vanish!

Who follows famous cats?

The pap-purr-azzi!

What do you call it when it's raining cats?

A down-purr!

What kind of music does an avocado listen to?

Guac and Roll!

What do you call an avocado in church?

Holy Guacamole!

What does a chili pepper say?

Brrrrrr!

What color balloons do you use
for a cheerleader's birthday party?

Yeller!

What kind of exercise is best for
a swimmer?

Pool-ups!

When does a joke become a
dad joke?

When it is fully groan!

What do you eat at a beach
party?

Sand-wiches!

Where does a unicorn go when
she loses a tail?

A retail store!

Why did the broom wake up late?

It over-swept!

What do you call an American bee?

USB!

How did the birthday banner feel
about where it was placed?

It was on the fence about it!

Why do moms make good
lacrosse players?

They are good at cradling!

Did you hear about the contest
for the best nail art?

It was a real nail biter!

Who is the funniest princess?

Ra-Pun-zel!!

Why did the girl put a ruler
in her sleeping bag?

To see how long she would sleep!

How do shoppers like their
eggs?

Money side up!

How can your ipad
help you fall asleep?

You must have a nap for that!

Why did Pegasus put clouds in her pancakes?

To make them light and fluffy!

Why shouldn't you invite a duck to a sleepover?

Because they wake up at the quack of dawn!

What do you call a dancing ghost?

Polka-haunt-us!

Why is it so easy to talk to Belle?

She is an open book!

How does Mom always seem to know what we are doing?

Because she sleeps with one eye open!

Why do birthday candles get
mad easily?

Because they have a short fuse!

What is a ballerina's favorite
breakfast?

A cinnamon bun!

Why was the girl such a hoot
at sleepover parties?

Because she was a night owl!

Who likes to hang
with their friends?

 Bats!

Why did the basketball player
bring an extra pair of
shoelaces to the game?

Because she wanted to tie
the score.

What kind of cheese does not
like to go to parties?

ProvAlone!

What is a horse rider's motto?

Helmet hair, don't care!

What does a cowgirl say when
she farts?

Darn tootin'!

What is Merida's favorite store?

Target!

How do you keep the breakfast bagels from getting away?

Put lox on them!

Where do ghosts play volleyball?

On a volleyball corpse!

What did the volleyball player name her dog?

Spike!

How does Grandma send a
Happy Birthday text?

Insta-gram!

Happy
Birthday!
Love,
Gram

Who needs a selfie stick to
take his birthday selfie?

T. Rex!

What happens if you
use a bag of ruffles
potato chips as a pillow?

You make head-lines!

Knock, knock.
Who's there?
Zinc.
Zinc who?

Do you Zinc we will get any
sleep tonight?!

What do trees put on their
birthday cakes?

Candle-sticks!

What game are unicorns really good at?

Ring toss with doughnuts!

How did the orange find room at the breakfast table?

It squeezed its way in!

How is a friend like a book?

You don't need to read them all,
you just pick the best ones!

Where does Alice go to play
question games?

Wonder-land!

Why did the lights stay on
all night?

Someone was asleep at the
switch!

Why did the astronaut want his own pillow fort?

Because he just needed a little space!

Why is it a good idea to invite unicorns to your party?

Because they like to poke fun with everyone!

What is Snow White's favorite store?

7-Eleven!

Why was the birthday candle
put in time out?

It had a meltdown!

Why don't mosquitoes play
hide and seek?

Noone will look for them!

What do you call a girl who likes
Christmas time sleepovers?

 Holly!

Why can't computers stay up
all night at slumber parties?

Because they crash!

What kind of fruit do you
eat at an outer space party?

Star-fruit!

Why do geese bring warm blankets
to sleepover parties?

Because they always get
goosebumps!

Why didn't the frog want to stay overnight at the sleepover?

Because he was a worrywart!

What do you call a cat that likes to talk a lot?

A gossip-purr!

Why are mermaids afraid of watching shows on their computer?

They are afraid of getting caught in Net-flix!

What does a llama princess
like to drink?

Royal tea!

Can you ask a pizza delivery person
for a funny sleepover joke?

Sure, he will deliver!

What did Ariel play with when she was little?

Doll-fins!

Why did the owl want to hang with her friends?

She didn't want to be owl by herself!

What kind of s'mores do you make
for a sleepover party?

A s'more-gasbord!

What is a gymnast's favorite
slumber party game?

Twister!

What do you call a jacket that
is on fire?

A blazer!

Why does Ariel live in saltwater?

Because pepper water would
make her sneeze!

What does a chicken wear
in her hair?

Eggstentions!

What new medical condition can
be attributed to the cellphone?

Selfie arm syndrome!

Why do party hats last a
long time?

Because you don't wear
them out!

What kind of cup can't you drink
out of?

A cupcake!

What candy is never at the
party on time?

Choco-late!

What do fairies make party
sandwiches with?

Shortbread!

Why didn't the kids laugh at the birthday banner joke?

It was over their head!

The party was so bummed that
they burned their Hawaiian pizza!

They should have cooked
it on aloha temperature!

Who doesn't like pizza?

A weird-dough!

Why did the blogger go to
the ice cream shop?

To get the scoop!

What should you drink before
you go on a trampoline?

Spring water!

How do you make really cool
hot dogs?

Add chilly peppers!

What kind of weather can you
create?

A brainstorm!

Knock, knock.
Who's there?
Colleen.
Colleen who?

Colleen all divas, it's time
to do our blind make-overs!

Knock, knock.
Who's there?
Stopwatch.
Stopwatch who?

Stopwatch you're doing and
lets have a pillow fight!

Knock, knock.
Who's there?
Butter.
Butter who?

We butter play Just Dance
before it gets too late!

Knock, knock.
Who's there?
Slumber.
Slumber who?

Slumber Party Hair, Don't Care!

Knock, knock.
Who's there?
Lettuce.
Lettuce who?

Lettuce know when we can
start turning up the music!

Knock, knock.
Who's there?
Usher.
Usher who?

Usher wish we could have
midnight munchies soon!

Knock, knock.
Who's there?
Police.
Police who?

Can we police do wacky hairstyles!

Knock, knock.
Who's there?
Radio.
Radio who?

Radio or not, it's time to tell ghost stories!

Knock, knock.
Who's there?
Juneau.
Juneau who?

Juneau who you want to
photobomb next?

Knock, knock.
Who's there?
Doughnut.
Doughnut who?

Doughnut worry, we will
play Questions Galore tonight!

Knock, knock.
Who's there?
Thor.
Thor who?

We are going to be Thor
after our dance party!

Knock, knock.
Who's there?
Irish.
Irish who?

Irish I packed my big unicorn
pillow for the party!

Knock, knock.
Who's there?
Justin.
Justin who?

Justin time to wake up
the Birthday girl!

Knock, knock.
Who's there?
Amoeba
Amoeba who?

Amoeba wrong, but I think I
see the sunrise!

We hope that your slumber party was filled with lots of extra fun and giggles with the Try Not to Laugh Challenge Sleepover Party Edition Joke Book!

Please consider leaving us a review on Amazon.com. We value your feedback & greatly appreciate your time!

Thank you

Howling Moon Books

Available from Howling Moon Books

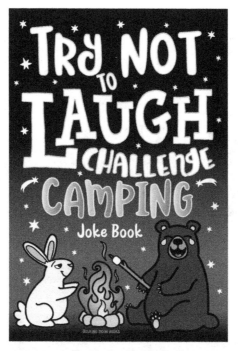

Also Available from Howling Moon Books

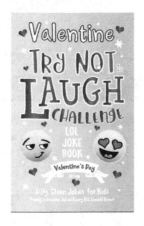

Also Available from Howling Moon Books

Made in the USA
Middletown, DE
12 June 2020